PRACTICAL MYSTICISM

EVELYN UNDERHILL (1875-1941), English poet, novelist and writer on mysticism, was born in England and educated at King's College for Women, London. In 1921 Miss Underhill was Upton Lecturer on the Philosophy of Religion at Manchester College, Oxford. Between 1900 and 1920 she wrote novels and light verse, but her lasting fame rests on the many books she produced on various aspects of mysticism. The most famous of these is *Mysticism* (1911). Among her other fine works in addition to *Practical Mysticism* are: *The Mystic Way* (1913), *The Essentials of Mysticism* (1920), *The Life of the Spirit and the Life of Today* (1922), *Concerning the Inner Light* (1926), *Man and the Supernatural* (1927) and *The House of the Soul* (1929).

PRACTICAL MYSTICISM was first published in 1915.

character. The real mystical life, which is the truly practical life, begins at the beginning; not with supernatural acts and ecstatic apprehensions, but with the normal faculties of the normal man. "I do not require of you," says Teresa to her pupils in meditation, "to form great and curious considerations in your understanding: I require of you no more than to *look*."

It might be thought that such looking at the spiritual world, simply, intensely, without cleverness—such an opening of the Eye of Eternity—was the essence of contemplation itself: and indeed one of the best definitions has described that art as a "loving sight," a "peering into heaven with the ghostly eye." But the self who is yet at this early stage of the pathway to Reality is not asked to look at anything new, to peer into the deeps of things: only to gaze with a new and cleansed vision on the ordinary intellectual images, the labels and the formulæ, the "objects" and ideas—even the external symbols—amongst which it has always dwelt. It is not yet advanced to the seeing of fresh landscapes: it is only able to re-examine the furniture of its home. and obtain from this exercise a skill, and a control of the attention, which shall afterwards be applied to greater purposes. Its task is here to *consider* that furniture, as the Victorines called this preliminary training: to take, that is, a more starry view of it: standing back from the whirl of the earth, and observing the process of things.

Take, then, an idea, an object, from amongst the common stock, and hold it before your mind. The selection is large enough: all sentient beings may find subjects of meditation to their taste, for there lies a universal behind every particular of thought, however concrete it may appear, and within the most rational propositions the meditative eye may glimpse a dream.

> "Reason has moons, but moons not hers
>   Lie mirror'd on her sea,
> Confounding her astronomers
>   But, O delighting me."

Even those objects which minister to our sense-life may well be used to nourish our spirits too. Who has not watched the intent meditations of a comfortable cat brooding upon the Absolute Mouse? You, if you have a philosophic twist, may transcend such relative views of Reality, and try to meditate on Time, Succession, even Being itself: or again on human intercourse, birth, growth, and death, on a flower, a river, the various tapestries of the sky. Even your own emotional life will provide you with the ideas of love, joy, peace, mercy, conflict, desire. You may range, with Kant, from the stars to the moral law. If your turn be to religion, the richest and most evocative of fields is open to your choice: from the plaster image to the mysteries of Faith.

But, the choice made, it must be held and defended during the time of meditation against all invasions from without, however insidious their encroachments, however "spiritual" their disguise. It must be brooded upon, gazed at, seized again and again, as distractions seem to snatch it from your grasp. A restless boredom, a dreary conviction of your own incapacity, will presently attack you. This, too, must be resisted at swordpoint. The first quarter of an hour thus spent in attempted meditation will be, indeed, a time of warfare; which should at least convince you how unruly, how ill-educated is your attention, how miserably ineffective your will, how far away you are from the captaincy of your own soul. It should convince, too, the most common-sense of philosophers of the distinction between real time, the true stream of duration which is life, and the sequence of seconds so carefully measured by the clock. Never before has the stream flowed so slowly, or fifteen minutes taken so long to pass. Consciousness has been lifted to a longer, slower rhythm, and is not yet adjusted to its solemn march.

But, striving for this new poise, intent on the achievement of it, presently it will happen to you to find that you have indeed—though how you know not—entered upon a fresh plane of perception, altered your relation with things.

First, the subject of your meditation begins, as you surrender to its influence, to exhibit unsuspected meaning, beauty, power. A perpetual growth of significance keeps pace with the increase of attention which you bring to bear on it; that attention which is the one agent of all your apprehensions, physical and mental alike. It ceases to be thin and abstract. You sink as it were into the deeps of it, rest in it, "unite" with it; and learn, in this still, intent communion, something of its depth and breadth and height, as we learn by direct intercourse to know our friends.

Moreover, as your meditation becomes deeper it will defend you from the perpetual assaults of the outer world. You will hear the busy hum of that world as a distant exterior melody, and know yourself to be in some sort withdrawn from it. You have set a ring of silence between you and it; and behold! within that silence you are free. You will look at the coloured scene, and it will seem to you thin and papery: only one amongst countless possible images of a deeper life as yet beyond your reach. And gradually, you will come to be aware of an entity, a *You*, who can thus hold at arm's length, be aware of, look at, an idea—a universe—other than itself. By this voluntary painful act of concentration, this first step upon the ladder which goes—as the mystics would say—from "multiplicity to unity," you have to some extent withdrawn yourself from that union with unrealities, with notions and concepts, which has hitherto contented you; and at once all the values of existence are changed. "The road to a Yea lies through a Nay." You, in this preliminary movement of recollection, are saying your first deliberate No to the claim which the world of appearance makes to a total possession of your consciousness: and are thus making possible some contact between that consciousness and the World of Reality.

Now turn this new purified and universalised gaze back upon yourself. Observe your own being in a fresh relation with things, and surrender yourself willingly to the moods of astonishment, humility, joy—perhaps of deep shame or sudden love—which invade your heart as you look. So doing patiently, day after day, constantly recapturing the vagrant attention, ever renewing the struggle for simplicity of sight, you will at last discover that there is something within you—something behind the fractious, conflicting life of desire—which you can recollect, gather up, make effective for new life. You will, in fact, know your own soul for the first time: and learn that there is a sense in which this real *You* is distinct from, an alien within, the world in which you find yourself, as an actor has another life when he is not on the stage. When you do not merely believe this but know it; when you have achieved this power of withdrawing yourself, of making this first crude distinction between appearance and reality, the initial stage of the contemplative life has been won. It is not much more of an achievement than that first proud effort in which the baby stands upright for a moment and then relapses to the more natural and convenient crawl: but it holds within it the same earnest of future development.

CHAPTER V

SELF-ADJUSTMENT

So, in a measure, you have found yourself: have retreated behind all that flowing appearance, that busy, unstable consciousness with its moods and obsessions, its feverish alternations of interest and apathy, its conflicts and irrational impulses, which even the psychologists mistake for You. Thanks to this recollective act, you have discovered in your inmost sanctuary a being not wholly practical, who refuses to be satisfied by your busy life of correspondences with the world of normal men, and hungers for communion with a spiritual universe. And this thing so foreign to your surface consciousness, yet familiar to it and continuous with it, you recognise as the true Self whose existence you always took for granted, but whom you have only known hitherto in its scattered manifestations. "That art thou."

This climb up the mountain of self-knowledge, said the Victorine mystics, is the necessary prelude to all illumination. Only at its summit do we discover, as Dante did, the beginning of the pathway to Reality. It is a lonely and an arduous excursion, a sufficient test of courage and sincerity: for most men prefer to dwell in comfortable ignorance upon the lower slopes, and there to make of their more obvious characteristics a drapery which shall veil the naked truth. True and complete self-knowledge, indeed, is the privilege of the strongest alone. Few can bear to contemplate themselves face to face; for the vision is strange and terrible, and brings awe and contrition in its wake. The life of the seer is changed by it for ever. He is converted, in the deepest and most drastic sense; is forced to take up a new attitude towards himself and all other things. Likely enough, if you really knew yourself—saw your own dim character, perpetually at the mercy of its environment; your true motives, stripped for inspection and measured against eternal values; your unacknowledged self-indulgences; your irrational loves and hates—you would be compelled to remodel your whole existence, and become for the first time a practical man.

But you have done what you can in this direction; have at last discovered your own deeper being, your eternal spark, the agent of all your contacts with Reality. You have often read about it. Now you have met it; know for a fact that it is there. What next? What changes, what readjustments will this self-revelation involve for you?

You will have noticed, as with practice your familiarity with the state of Recollection has increased, that the kind of consciousness which it brings with it, the sort of attitude which it demands of you, conflict sharply with the consciousness and the attitude which you have found so appropriate to your ordinary life in the past. They make this old attitude appear childish, unworthy, at last absurd. By this first deliberate effort to attend to Reality you are at once brought face to face with that dreadful revelation of disharmony, unrealness, and interior muddle which the blunt moralists call "conviction of sin." Never again need those moralists point out to you the inherent silliness of your earnest pursuit of impermanent things: your solemn concentration upon the game of getting on. None the less, this attitude persists. Again and again you swing back to it. Something more than realisation is needed if you are to adjust yourself to your new vision of the world. This game which you have played so long has formed and conditioned you, developing certain qualities and perceptions, leaving the rest in abeyance: so that now, suddenly asked to play another, which demands fresh movements, alertness of a different sort, your mental muscles are intractable, your attention refuses to respond. Nothing less will serve you here than that drastic remodelling of character which the mystics call "Purgation," the second stage in the training of the human consciousness for participation in Reality.

It is not merely that your intellect has assimilated, united with a superficial and unreal view of the world. Far worse: your will, your desire, the sum total of your energy, has been turned the wrong way, harnessed to the wrong machine. You have become accustomed to the idea that you want, or ought to want, certain valueless things, certain specific positions. For years your treasure

has been in the Stock Exchange, or the House of
Commons, or the Salon, or the reviews that "really
count" (if they still exist), or the drawing-rooms
of Mayfair; and thither your heart perpetually
tends to stray.   Habit has you in its chains.   You
are not free.   The awakening, then, of your
deeper self, which knows not habit and desires
nothing but free correspondence with the Real,
awakens you at once to the fact of a disharmony
between the simple but inexorable longings and
instincts of the buried spirit, now beginning to
assert themselves in your hours of meditation—
pushing out, as it were, towards the light—and
the various changeful, but insistent longings and
instincts of the surface-self.   Between these two
no peace is possible: they conflict at every turn.
It becomes apparent to you that the declaration
of Plotinus, accepted or repeated by all the mystics, concerning a "higher" and a "lower" life,
and the cleavage that exists between them, has a
certain justification even in the experience of the
ordinary man.

That great thinker and ecstatic said, that all
human personality was thus two-fold: thus capa-

ble of correspondence with two orders of existence. The "higher life" was always tending towards union with Reality; towards the gathering of itself up into One. The "lower life," framed for correspondence with the outward world of multiplicity, was always tending to fall downwards, and fritter the powers of the self among external things. This is but a restatement, in terms of practical existence, of the fact which Recollection brought home to us: that the human self is transitional, neither angel nor animal, capable of living towards either Eternity or Time. But it is one thing to frame beautiful theories on these subjects: another when the unresolved dualism of your own personality (though you may not give it this high-sounding name) becomes the main fact of consciousness, perpetually reasserts itself as a vital problem, and refuses to take academic rank.

This state of things means the acute discomfort which ensues on being pulled two ways at once. The uneasy swaying of attention between two incompatible ideals, the alternating conviction that there is something wrong, perverse, poisonous, about life as you have always lived it, and something hopelessly ethereal about the life which your innermost inhabitant wants to live—these disagreeable sensations grow stronger and stronger. First one and then the other asserts itself. You fluctuate miserably between their attractions and their claims; and will have no peace until these claims have been met, and the apparent opposition between them resolved. You are sure now that there is another, more durable and more "reasonable," life possible to the human consciousness than that on which it usually spends itself. But it is also clear to you that you must yourself be something more, or other, than you are now, if you are to achieve this life, dwell in it, and breathe its air. You have had in your brief spells of recollection a first quick vision of that plane of being which Augustine called "the land of peace," the "beauty old and new." You know for evermore that it exists: that the real thing within yourself belongs to it, might live in it, is being all the time invited and enticed to it. You begin, in fact, to feel and know in every fibre of your being the mystical need of "union with Reality"; and to realise that the natural scene which you have accepted so trustfully cannot provide the correspondences toward which you are stretching out.

Nevertheless, it is to correspondences with this natural order that you have given for many years your full attention, your desire, your will. The surface-self, left for so long in undisputed possession of the conscious field, has grown strong, and cemented itself like a limpet to the rock of the obvious; gladly exchanging freedom for apparent security, and building up, from a selection amongst the more concrete elements offered it by the rich stream of life, a defensive shell of "fixed ideas." It is useless to speak kindly to the limpet. You must detach it by main force. That old comfortable clinging life, protected by its hard shell from the living waters of the sea, must now come to an end. A conflict of some kind—a severance of old habits, old notions, old prejudices —is here inevitable for you; and a decision as to the form which the new adjustments must take.

Now although in a general way we may regard the practical man's attitude to existence as a limpet-like adherence to the unreal; yet, from an-

other point of view, fixity of purpose and desire
is the last thing we can attribute to him.   His
mind is full of little whirlpools, twists and currents, conflicting systems, incompatible desires.
One after another, he centres himself on ambition,
love, duty, friendship, social convention, politics,
religion, self-interest in one of its myriad forms;
making of each a core round which whole sections
of his life are arranged.   One after another, these
things either fail him or enslave him.   Sometimes
they become obsessions, distorting his judgment,
narrowing his outlook, colouring his whole existence.   Sometimes they develop inconsistent characters which involve him in public difficulties,
private compromises and self-deceptions of every
kind.   They split his attention, fritter his powers.
This state of affairs, which usually passes for an
"active life," begins to take on a different com-
plexion when looked at with the simple eye of
meditation.   Then we observe that the plain
man's world is in a muddle, just because he has
tried to arrange its major interests round himself
as round a centre; and he is neither strong enough
nor clever enough for the job.   He has made a

wretched little whirlpool in the mighty River of Becoming, interrupting—as he imagines, in his own interest—its even flow: and within that whirlpool are numerous petty complexes and counter-currents, amongst which his will and attention fly to and fro in a continual state of unrest. The man who makes a success of his life, in any department, is he who has chosen one from amongst these claims and interests, and devoted to it his energetic powers of heart and will; "unifying" himself about it, and from within it resisting all counter-claims. He has one objective, one centre; has killed out the lesser ones, and simplified himself.

Now the artist, the discoverer, the philosopher, the lover, the patriot—the true enthusiast for any form of life—can only achieve the full reality to which his special art or passion gives access by innumerable renunciations. He must kill out the smaller centres of interest, in order that his whole will, love, and attention may pour itself out towards, seize upon, unite with, that special manifestation of the beauty and significance of the universe to which he is drawn. So, too, a deliberate self-simplification, a "purgation" of the heart and will, is demanded of those who would develop the form of consciousness called "mystical." All your power, all your resolution, is needed if you are to succeed in this adventure: there must be no frittering of energy, no mixture of motives. We hear much of the mystical temperament, the mystical vision. The mystical character is far more important: and its chief ingredients are courage, singleness of heart, and self-control. It is towards the perfecting of these military virtues, not to the production of a pious softness, that the discipline of asceticism is largely directed; and the ascetic foundation, in one form or another, is the only enduring foundation of a sane contemplative life.

You cannot, until you have steadied yourself, found a poise, and begun to resist some amongst the innumerable claims which the world of appearance perpetually makes upon your attention and your desire, make much use of the new power which Recollection has disclosed to you; and this Recollection itself, so long as it remains merely a matter of attention and does not involve the heart, is no better than a psychic trick. You are committed therefore, as the fruit of your first attempts at self-knowledge, to a deliberate—probably a difficult—rearrangement of your character; to the stern course of self-discipline, the voluntary acts of choice on the one hand and of rejection on the other, which ascetic writers describe under the formidable names of Detachment and Mortification. By Detachment they mean the eviction of the limpet from its crevice; the refusal to anchor yourself to material things, to regard existence from the personal standpoint, or confuse custom with necessity. By Mortification, they mean the resolving of the turbulent whirlpools and currents of your own conflicting passions, interests, desires; the killing out of all those tendencies which the peaceful vision of Recollection would condemn, and which create the fundamental opposition between your interior and exterior life.

What then, in the last resort, is the source of this opposition; the true reason of your uneasiness, your unrest? The reason lies, not in any real incompatibility between the interests of the temporal and the eternal orders; which are but two

aspects of one Fact, two expressions of one Love.
It lies solely in yourself; in your attitude towards
the world of things.   You are enslaved by the
verb "to have": all your reactions to life consist in
corporate or individual demands, appetites, wants.
That "love of life" of which we sometimes speak
is mostly cupboard-love.   We are quick to snap
at her ankles when she locks the larder door: a
proceeding which we dignify by the name of
pessimism.   The mystic knows not this attitude
of demand.   He tells us again and again, that
"he is rid of all his asking"; that "henceforth the
heat of having shall never scorch him more."
Compare this with your normal attitude to the
world, practical man: your quiet certitude that
you are well within your rights in pushing the
claims of "the I, the Me, the Mine"; your habit,
if you be religious, of asking for the weather and
the government that you want, of persuading the
Supernal Powers to take a special interest in your
national or personal health and prosperity.   How
often in each day do you deliberately revert to an
attitude of disinterested adoration?   Yet this is
the only attitude in which true communion with

the universe is possible. The very mainspring of your activity is a demand, either for a continued possession of that which you have, or for something which as yet you have not: wealth, honour, success, social position, love, friendship, comfort, amusement. You feel that you have a right to some of these things: to a certain recognition of your powers, a certain immunity from failure or humiliation. You resent anything which opposes you in these matters. You become restless when you see other selves more skilful in the game of acquisition than yourself. You hold tight against all comers your own share of the spoils. You are rather inclined to shirk boring responsibilities and unattractive, unremunerative toil; are greedy of pleasure and excitement, devoted to the art of having a good time. If you possess a social sense, you demand these things not only for yourself but for your tribe—the domestic or racial group to which you belong. These dispositions, so ordinary that they almost pass unnoticed, were named by our blunt forefathers the Seven Deadly Sins of Pride, Anger, Envy, Avarice, Sloth, Gluttony, and Lust. Per-

haps you would rather call them—as indeed they
are—the seven common forms of egotism. They
represent the natural reactions to life of the self-
centred human consciousness, enslaved by the
"world of multiplicity"; and constitute absolute
barriers to its attainment of Reality. So long as
these dispositions govern character we can never
see or feel things as they are; but only as they
affect ourselves, our family, our party, our business, our church, our empire—the I, the Me, the
Mine, in its narrower or wider manifestations.
Only the detached and purified heart can view all
things—the irrational cruelty of circumstance, the
tortures of war, the apparent injustice of life, the
acts and beliefs of enemy and friend—in true proportion; and reckon with calm mind the sum of
evil and good. Therefore the mystics tell us perpetually that "selfhood must be killed" before
Reality can be attained.

"Feel sin a lump, thou wottest never what, but
none other thing than *thyself*," says *The Cloud of
Unknowing*. "When the I, the Me, and the
Mine are dead, the work of the Lord is done,"
says Kabir. The substance of that wrongness of

act and relation which constitutes "sin" is the separation of the individual spirit from the whole; the ridiculous megalomania which makes each man the centre of his universe. Hence comes the turning inwards and condensation of his energies and desires, till they do indeed form a "lump"; a hard, tight core about which all the currents of his existence swirl. This heavy weight within the heart resists every outgoing impulse of the spirit; and tends to draw all things inward and downward to itself, never to pour itself forth in love, enthusiasm, sacrifice. "So long," says the *Theologia Germanica*, "as a man seeketh his own will and his own highest good, because it is his, and for his own sake, he will never find it: for so long as he doeth this, he is not seeking his own highest good, and how then should he find it? For so long as he doeth this, he seeketh himself, and dreameth that he is himself the highest good. . . . But whosoever seeketh, loveth, and pursueth goodness, as goodness and for the sake of goodness, and maketh that his end—for nothing but the love of goodness, not for love of the I, Me, Mine, Self, and the like—he will find the highest good, for he seeketh it aright, and they who seek it otherwise do err."

So it is disinterestedness, the saint's and poet's love of things for their own sakes, the vision of the charitable heart, which is the secret of union with Reality and the condition of all real knowledge. This brings with it the precious quality of suppleness, the power of responding with ease and simplicity to the great rhythms of life; and this will only come when the ungainly "lump" of sin is broken, and the verb "to have," which expresses its reaction to existence, is ejected from the centre of your consciousness. Then your attitude to life will cease to be commercial, and become artistic. Then the guardian at the gate, scrutinising and sorting the incoming impressions, will no longer ask, "What use is this to *me?*" before admitting the angel of beauty or significance who demands your hospitality. Then things will cease to have power over you. You will become free. "Son," says à Kempis, "thou oughtest diligently to attend to this; that in every place, every action or outward occupation, thou be inwardly free and mighty in thyself, and all things be under thee, and thou not under them; that thou be lord and governor of thy deeds, not servant."

It is therefore by the withdrawal of your will from its feverish attachment to things, till "they are under thee and thou not under them," that you will gradually resolve the opposition between the recollective and the active sides of your personality. By diligent self-discipline, that mental attitude which the mystics sometimes call poverty and sometimes perfect freedom—for these are two aspects of one thing—will become possible to you. Ascending the mountain of self-knowledge and throwing aside your superfluous luggage as you go, you shall at last arrive at the point which they call the summit of the spirit; where the various forces of your character—brute energy, keen intellect, desirous heart—long dissipated amongst a thousand little wants and preferences, are gathered into one, and become a strong and disciplined instrument wherewith your true self can force a path deeper and deeper into the heart of Reality.

CHAPTER VI

LOVE AND WILL

THIS steady effort towards the simplifying of your tangled character, its gradual emancipation from the fetters of the unreal, is not to dispense you from that other special training of the attention which the diligent practice of meditation and recollection effects. Your pursuit of the one must never involve neglect of the other; for these are the two sides—one moral, the other mental—of that unique process of self-conquest which Ruysbroeck calls "the gathering of the forces of the soul into the unity of the spirit": the welding together of all your powers, the focussing of them upon one point. Hence they should never, either in theory or practice, be separated. Only the act of recollection, the constantly renewed retreat to the quiet centre of the spirit, gives that assurance of a Reality, a calmer and more valid life attainable by us, which supports the stress and pain of self-simplification and permits us to hope on, even in the teeth of the world's cruelty, indifference, degeneracy; whilst diligent character-building alone, with its perpetual untiring efforts at self-adjustment, its bracing, purging discipline, checks the human tendency to relapse into and react to the obvious, and makes possible the further development of the contemplative power.

So it is through and by these two great changes in your attitude towards things—first, the change of attention, which enables you to perceive a truer universe; next, the deliberate rearrangement of your ideas, energies, and desires in harmony with that which you have seen—that a progressive uniformity of life and experience is secured to you, and you are defended against the dangers of an indolent and useless mysticality. Only the real, say the mystics, can know Reality, for "we behold that which we are," the universe which we see is conditioned by the character of the mind that sees it: and this realness—since that which you seek is no mere glimpse of Eternal Life, but complete possession of it—must apply to every aspect of your being, the rich totality of character, all the "forces of the soul," not to some thin and isolated "spiritual sense" alone. This is why recollection and self-simplification—perception of, and adaptation to, the Spiritual World in which we dwell—are the essential preparations for the mystical life, and neither can exist in a wholesome and well-balanced form without the other. By them the mind, the will, the heart, which so long had dissipated their energies over a thousand scattered notions, wants, and loves, are gradually detached from their old exclusive pre-occupation with the ephemeral interests of the self, or of the group to which the self belongs.

You, if you practise them, will find after a time —perhaps a long time—that the hard work which they involve has indeed brought about a profound and definite change in you. A new suppleness has taken the place of that rigidity which you have been accustomed to mistake for strength of character: an easier attitude towards the accidents of life. Your whole scale of values has undergone a silent transformation, since you have ceased to fight for your own hand and regard the nearest-at-hand world as the only one that counts. You have become, as the mystics would say, "free from inordinate attachments," the "heat of having" does not scorch you any more; and because of this you possess great inward liberty, a sense of spaciousness and peace. Released from the obsessions which so long had governed them, will, heart, and mind are now all bent to the purposes of your deepest being: "gathered in the unity of the spirit," they have fused to become an agent with which it can act.

What form, then, shall this action take? It shall take a practical form, shall express itself in terms of movement: the pressing outwards of the whole personality, the eager and trustful stretching of it towards the fresh universe which awaits you. As all scattered thinking was cut off in recollection, as all vagrant and unworthy desires have been killed by the exercises of detachment; so now all scattered willing, all hesitations between the indrawing and outflowing instincts of the soul, shall be checked and resolved. You are to *push* with all your power: not to absorb ideas, but to pour forth will and love. With this "conative act," as the psychologists would call it, the true contemplative life begins. Contempla-

tion, you see, has no very close connection with
dreaminess and idle musing: it is more like the intense effort of vision, the passionate and self-
forgetful act of communion, presupposed in all
creative art.   It is, says one old English mystic,
"a blind intent stretching . . . a privy love
pressed" in the direction of Ultimate Beauty,
athwart all the checks, hindrances, and contradic-
tions of the restless world: a "loving stretching
out" towards Reality, says the great Ruysbroeck,
than whom none has gone further on this path.
Tension, ardour, are of its essence: it demands the
perpetual exercise of industry and courage.

We observe in such definitions as these a strange
neglect of that glory of man, the Pure Intellect,
with which the spiritual prig enjoys to believe
that he can climb up to the Empyrean itself.   It
almost seems as though the mystics shared Keats'
view of the supremacy of feeling over thought;
and reached out towards some new and higher
range of sensation, rather than towards new and
more accurate ideas.   They are ever eager to as-
sure us that man's most sublime thoughts of the
Transcendent are but a little better than his

worst: that loving intuition is the only certain
guide. "By love may He be gotten and holden,
but by thought never."

Yet here you are not to fall into the clumsy
error of supposing that the things which are beyond the grasp of reason are necessarily unrea-
sonable things. Immediate feeling, so far as it is
true, does not oppose but transcends and completes the highest results of thought. It contains
within itself the sum of all the processes through
which thought would pass in the act of attaining
the same goal: supposing thought to have reached
—as it has not—the high pitch at which it was
capable of thinking its way all along this road.

In the preliminary act of gathering yourself
together, and in those unremitting explorations
through which you came to "a knowing and a
feeling of yourself as you are," thought assuredly
had its place. There the powers of analysis,
criticism, and deduction found work that they
could do. But now it is the love and will—the
feeling, the intent, the passionate desire—of the
self, which shall govern your activities and make
possible your success. Few would care to brave

the horrors of a courtship conducted upon strictly intellectual lines: and contemplation is an act of love, the wooing, not the critical study, of Divine Reality. It is an eager outpouring of ourselves towards a Somewhat Other for which we feel a passion of desire; a seeking, touching, and tasting, not a considering and analysing, of the beautiful and true wherever found. It is, as it were, a responsive act of the organism to those Supernal Powers without, which touch and stir it. Deep humility as towards those Powers, a willing surrender to their control, is the first condition of success. The mystics speak much of these elusive contacts; felt more and more in the soul, as it becomes increasingly sensitive to the subtle movements of its spiritual environment.

> "Sense, feeling, taste, complacency, and sight,
>   These are the true and real joys,
>   The living, flowing, inward, melting, bright
>   And heavenly pleasures; all the rest are toys;
>   All which are founded in Desire
>   As light in flame and heat in fire."

But this new method of correspondence with the universe is not to be identified with "mere feeling" in its lowest and least orderly forms. Contemplation does not mean abject surrender to every "mystical" impression that comes in. It is no sentimental æstheticism or emotional piety to which you are being invited: nor shall the transcending of reason ever be achieved by way of spiritual silliness. All the powers of the self, raised to their intensest form, shall be used in it; though used perhaps in a new way. These, the three great faculties of love, thought, and will —with which you have been accustomed to make great show on the periphery of consciousness— you have, as it were, drawn inwards during the course of your inward retreat: and by your education in detachment have cured them of their tendency to fritter their powers amongst a multiplicity of objects. Now, at the very heart of personality, you are alone with them; you hold with you in that "Interior Castle," and undistracted for the moment by the demands of practical existence, the three great tools wherewith the soul deals with life.

As regards the life you have hitherto looked upon as "normal," love—understood in its widest

sense, as desire, emotional inclination—has
throughout directed your activities. You did
things, sought things, learned things, even suffered
things, because at bottom you wanted to. Will
has done the work to which love spurred it:
thought has assimilated the results of their activities and made for them pictures, analyses, "ex-
planations" of the world with which they had to
deal. But now your purified love discerns and
desires, your will is set towards, something which
thought cannot really assimilate—still less ex-
plain. "Contemplation," says Ruysbroeck, "is a
knowing that is in no wise . . . therein all the
workings of the reason fail." That reason has
been trained to deal with the stuff of temporal
existence. It will only make mincemeat of your
experience of Eternity if you give it a chance;
trimming, transforming, rationalising that ineffable vision, trying to force it into a symbolic system with which the intellect can cope. This is
why the great contemplatives utter again and
again their solemn warning against the deceptive-
ness of thought when it ventures to deal with the
spiritual intuitions of man; crying with the author

of *The Cloud of Unknowing*, "Look that *nothing* live in thy working mind but a naked intent stretching"—the voluntary tension of your ever-growing, ever-moving personality pushing out towards the Real. "Love, and *do* what you like," said the wise Augustine: so little does mere surface activity count, against the deep motive that begets it.

The dynamic power of love and will, the fact that the heart's desire—if it be intense and industrious—is a better earnest of possible fulfilment than the most elegant theories of the spiritual world; this is the perpetual theme of all the Christian mystics. By such love, they think, the worlds themselves were made. By an eager outstretching towards Reality, they tell us, we tend to move towards Reality, to enter into its rhythm: by a humble and unquestioning surrender to it we permit its entrance into our souls. This twofold act, in which we find the double character of all true love—which both gives and takes, yields and demands—is assured, if we be patient and single-hearted, of ultimate success. At last our ignorance shall be done away; and we shall "appre-

hend" the real and the eternal, as we apprehend
the sunshine when the sky is free from cloud.
Therefore "Smite upon that thick cloud of unknowing with a sharp dart of longing love"—and
suddenly it shall part, and disclose the blue.

"Smite," "press," "push," "strive"—these are
strong words: yet they are constantly upon the
lips of the contemplatives when describing the
earlier stages of their art.   Clearly, the abolition
of discursive thought is not to absolve you from
the obligations of industry.   You are to "ener-
gise enthusiastically" upon new planes, where
you shall see more intensely, hear more intensely,
touch and taste more intensely than ever before:
for the modes of communion which these senses
make possible to you are now to operate as parts
of the one single state of perfect intuition, of loving knowledge by union, to which you are growing up.   And gradually you come to see that, if
this be so, it is the ardent will that shall be the
prime agent of your undertaking: a will which has
now become the active expression of your deepest
and purest desires.   About this the recollected
and simplified self is to gather itself as a centre;

and thence to look out—steadily, deliberately—
with eyes of love towards the world.

To "look with the eyes of love" seems a vague
and sentimental recommendation: yet the whole
art of spiritual communion is summed in it, and
exact and important results flow from this exercise.   The attitude which it involves is an attitude of complete humility and of receptiveness;
without criticism, without clever analysis of the
thing seen.   When you look thus, you surrender
your I-hood; see things at last as the artist does,
for their sake, not for your own.   The fundamental unity that is in you reaches out to the
unity that is in them: and you achieve the
"Simple Vision" of the poet and the mystic—
that synthetic and undistorted apprehension of
things which is the antithesis of the single vision
of practical men.   The doors of perception are
cleansed, and everything appears as it is.   The
disfiguring results of hate, rivalry, prejudice, vanish away.   Into that silent place to which recollection has brought you, new music, new colour,
new light, are poured from the outward world.

The conscious love which achieves this vision

may, indeed must, fluctuate—"As long as thou livest thou art subject to mutability; yea, though thou wilt not!" But the *will* which that love has enkindled can hold attention in the right direction. It can refuse to relapse to unreal and egotistic correspondences; and continue, even in darkness, and in the suffering which such darkness brings to the awakened spirit, its appointed task, cutting a way into new levels of Reality.

Therefore this transitional stage in the development of the contemplative powers—in one sense the completion of their elementary schooling, in another the beginning of their true activities—is concerned with the toughening and further training of that will which self-simplification has detached from its old concentration upon the unreal wants and interests of the self. Merged with your intuitive love, this is to become the true agent of your encounter with Reality; for that Simple Eye of Intention, which is so supremely your own, and in the last resort the maker of your universe and controller of your destiny, is nothing else but a synthesis of such energetic will and such uncorrupt desire, turned and held in the direction of the Best.

CHAPTER VII

THE FIRST FORM OF CONTEMPLATION

CONCENTRATION, recollection, a profound self-criticism, the stilling of his busy surface-intellect, his restless emotions of enmity and desire, the voluntary achievement of an attitude of disinterested love—by these strange paths the practical man has now been led, in order that he may know by communion something of the greater Life in which he is immersed and which he has so long and so successfully ignored. He has managed in his own small way something equivalent to those drastic purifications, those searching readjustments, which are undertaken by the heroic seekers for Reality; the arts whereby they defeat the tyranny of "the I, the Me, the Mine" and achieve the freedom of a wider life. Now, perhaps, he may share to some extent in that illumination, that extended and intensified perception of things, which they declare to be the heritage of the liberated consciousness.

This illumination shall be gradual. The attainment of it depends not so much upon a philosophy accepted, or a new gift of vision suddenly received, as upon an uninterrupted changing and widening of character; a progressive growth towards the Real, an ever more profound harmonisation of the self's life with the greater and inclusive rhythms of existence. It shall therefore develop in width and depth as the sphere of that self's intuitive love extends. As your own practical sympathy with and understanding of other lives, your realisation of them, may be narrowed and stiffened to include no more than the family group, or spread over your fellow-workers, your class, your city, party, country, or religion —even perhaps the whole race—till you feel yourself utterly part of it, moving with it, suffering with it, and partake of its whole conscious life; so here. Self-mergence is a gradual process, dependent on a progressive unlimiting of personality. The apprehension of Reality which rewards it is gradual too. In essence, it is one continuous out-flowing movement towards that boundless heavenly consciousness where the "flaming ramparts" which shut you from true communion with all other selves and things is done away; an unbroken process of expansion and simplification, which is nothing more or less than the growth of the spirit of love, the full flowering of the patriotic sense. By this perpetually-renewed casting down of the hard barriers of individuality, these willing submissions to the compelling rhythm of a larger existence than that of the solitary individual or even of the human group— by this perpetual widening, deepening, and unselfing of your attentiveness—you are to enlarge your boundaries and become the citizen of a greater, more joyous, more poignant world, the partaker of a more abundant life. The limits of this enlargement have not yet been discovered. The greatest contemplatives, returning from their highest ascents, can only tell us of a world that is "unwalled."

But this growth into higher realities, this blossoming of your contemplative consciousness— though it be, like all else we know in life, an unbroken process of movement and change—must be broken up and reduced to the series of concrete forms which we call "order" if our inelastic minds are to grasp it. So, we will consider it as the successive achievement of those three levels or manifestations of Reality, which we have agreed to call the Natural World of Becoming, the Metaphysical World of Being, and—last and highest—that Divine Reality within which these opposites are found as one. Though these three worlds of experience are so plaited together, that intimations from the deeper layers of being constantly reach you through the natural scene, it is in this order of realisation that you may best think of them, and of your own gradual upgrowth to the full stature of humanity. To elude nature, to refuse her friendship, and attempt to leap the river of life in the hope of finding God on the other side, is the common error of a perverted mysticality. It is as fatal in result as the opposite error of deliberately arrested development, which, being attuned to the wonderful rhythms of natural life, is content with this increase of sensibility; and, becoming a "nature-mystic," asks no more.

So you are to begin with that first form of contemplation which the old mystics sometimes called the "discovery of God in His creatures." Not with some ecstatic adventure in supersensuous regions, but with the loving and patient exploration of the world that lies at your gates; the "ebb and flow and ever-during power" of which your own existence forms a part. You are to push back the self's barriers bit by bit, till at last all duration is included in the widening circles of its intuitive love: till you find in every manifestation of life—even those which you have petulantly classified as cruel or obscene—the ardent self-expression of that Immanent Being whose spark burns deep in your own soul.

The Indian mystics speak perpetually of the visible universe as the *Līlā* or Sport of God: the Infinite deliberately expressing Himself in finite form, the musical manifestation of His creative joy. All gracious and all courteous souls, they think, will gladly join His play; considering rather the wonder and achievement of the whole —its vivid movement, its strange and terrible evocations of beauty from torment, nobility from conflict and death, its mingled splendour of

sacrifice and triumph—than their personal con-
quests, disappointments, and fatigues. In the
first form of contemplation you are to realise the
movement of this game, in which you have played
so long a languid and involuntary part, and find
your own place in it. It is flowing, growing,
changing, making perpetual unexpected patterns
within the evolving melody of the Divine
Thought. In all things it is incomplete, unstable;
and so are you. Your fellow-men, enduring on
the battlefield, living and breeding in the slum,
adventurous and studious, sensuous and pure—
more, your great comrades, the hills, the trees,
the rivers, the darting birds, the scuttering insects,
the little soft populations of the grass—all these
are playing with you. They move one to another
in delicate responsive measures, now violent, now
gentle, now in conflict, now in peace; yet ever
weaving the pattern of a ritual dance, and obedi-
ent to the music of that invisible Choragus whom
Boehme and Plotinus knew. What is that great
wind which blows without, in continuous and
ineffable harmonies? Part of you, practical man.
There is but one music in the world: and to it

you contribute perpetually, whether you will or
no, your one little ditty of no tone.

"Mad with joy, life and death dance to the rhythm of this
        music:
The hills and the sea and the earth dance:
The world of man dances in laughter and tears."

It seems a pity to remain in ignorance of this, to
keep as it were a plate-glass window between
yourself and your fellow-dancers—all those other
thoughts of God, perpetually becoming, changing
and growing beside you—and commit yourself to
the unsocial attitude of the "cat that walks by
itself."

   Begin therefore at once.   Gather yourself up,
as the exercises of recollection have taught you to
do.   Then—with attention no longer frittered
amongst the petty accidents and interests of your
personal life, but poised, tense, ready for the work
you shall demand of it—stretch out by a distinct
act of loving will towards one of the myriad
manifestations of life that surround you: and
which, in an ordinary way, you hardly notice
unless you happen to need them.   Pour yourself
out towards it, do not draw its image towards

you. Deliberate—more, impassioned—attentiveness, an attentiveness which soon transcends all
consciousness of yourself, as separate from and
attending to the thing seen; this is the condition
of success. As to the object of contemplation,
it matters little. From Alp to insect, anything
will do, provided that your attitude be right:
for all things in this world towards which you
are stretching out are linked together, and one
truly apprehended will be the gateway to the
rest.

Look with the eye of contemplation on the
most dissipated tabby of the streets, and you shall
discern the celestial quality of life set like an
aureole about his tattered ears, and hear in his
strident mew an echo of

> "The deep enthusiastic joy,
> The rapture of the hallelujah sent
> From all that breathes and is."

The sooty tree up which he scrambles to escape
your earnest gaze is holy too. It contains for you
the whole divine cycle of the seasons; upon the
plane of quiet, its inward pulse is clearly to be
heard. But you must look at these things as you

would look into the eyes of a friend: ardently, selflessly, without considering his reputation, his practical uses, his anatomical peculiarities, or the vices which might emerge were he subjected to psycho-analysis.

Such a simple exercise, if entered upon with singleness of heart, will soon repay you. By this quiet yet tense act of communion, this loving gaze, you will presently discover a relationship— far more intimate than anything you imagined— between yourself and the surrounding "objects of sense"; and in those objects of sense a profound significance, a personal quality, and actual power of response, which you might in cooler moments think absurd. Making good your correspond-ences with these fellow-travellers, you will learn to say with Whitman:

"You air that serves me with breath to speak!
You objects that call from diffusion my meanings and
    give them shape!
You light that wraps me and all things in delicate
    equable showers!
You paths worn in the irregular hollows by the roadside!
I believe you are latent with unseen existences, you are
    so dear to me."

A subtle interpenetration of your spirit with the spirit of those "unseen existences," now so deeply and thrillingly felt by you, will take place. Old barriers will vanish: and you will become aware that St. Francis was accurate as well as charming when he spoke of Brother Wind and Sister Water; and that Stevenson was obviously right when he said, that since

> "The world is so full of a number of things,
> I'm sure we ought all to be happy as kings."

Those glad and vivid "things" will speak to you. They will offer you news at least as definite and credible as that which the paper-boy is hawking in the street: direct messages from that Beauty which the artist reports at best at second hand. Because of your new sensitiveness, anthems will be heard of you from every gutter; poems of intolerable loveliness will bud for you on every weed. Best and greatest, your fellow-men will shine for you with new significance and light. Humility and awe will be evoked in you by the beautiful and patient figures of the poor, their long dumb heroisms, their willing acceptance of the burden of life. All the various members of the human group, the little children and the aged, those who stand for energy, those dedicated to skill, to thought, to plainest service, or to prayer, will have for you fresh vivid significance, be felt as part of your own wider being. All adventurous endeavours, all splendour of pain and all beauty of play—more, that grey unceasing effort of existence which makes up the groundwork of the social web, and the ineffective hopes, enthusiasms, and loves which transfuse it—all these will be seen and felt by you at last as full of glory, full of meaning; for you will see them with innocent, attentive, disinterested eyes, feel them as infinitely significant and adorable parts of the Transcendent Whole in which you also are immersed.

This discovery of your fraternal link with all living things, this down-sinking of your arrogant personality into the great generous stream of life, marks an important stage in your apprehension of that Science of Love which contemplation is to teach. You are not to confuse it with pretty fancies about nature, such as all imaginative persons enjoy; still less, with a self-conscious and deliberate humanitarianism. It is a veritable condition of awareness; a direct perception, not an opinion or an idea. For those who attain it, the span of the senses is extended. These live in a world which is lit with an intenser light; has, as George Fox insisted, "another smell than before." They hear all about them the delicate music of growth, and see the "new colour" of which the mystics speak.

Further, you will observe that this act, and the attitude which is proper to it, differs in a very important way even from that special attentiveness which characterised the stage of meditation, and which seems at first sight to resemble it in many respects. Then, it was an idea or image from amongst the common stock—one of those conceptual labels with which the human paste-brush has decorated the surface of the universe—which you were encouraged to hold before your mind. Now, turning away from the label, you shall surrender yourself to the direct message poured out towards you by the *thing*. Then, you considered: now, you are to absorb. This experience

will be, in the very highest sense, the experience
of sensation without thought: the essential sensation, the "savouring" to which some of the mystics
invite us, of which our fragmentary bodily senses
offer us a transient sacrament. So here at last,
in this intimate communion, this "simple seeing,"
this total surrender of you to the impress of things,
you are using to the full the sacred powers of
sense: and so using them, because you are con-
centrating upon them, accepting their reports in
simplicity. You have, in this contemplative
outlook, carried the peculiar methods of artistic
apprehension to their highest stage: with the result
that the sense-world has become for you, as
Erigena said that all creatures were, "a theophany,
or appearance of God." Not, you observe, a
symbol, but a showing: a very different thing.
You have begun now the Plotinian ascent from
multiplicity to unity, and therefore begin to perceive in the Many the clear and actual presence
of the One: the changeless and absolute Life,
manifesting itself in all the myriad nascent, cres-
cent, cadent lives. Poets, gazing thus at the
"flower in the crannied wall" or the "green thing

that stands in the way," have been led deep into the heart of its life; there to discern the secret of the universe.

All the greater poems of Wordsworth and Walt Whitman represent an attempt to translate direct contemplative experience of this kind into words and rhythms which might convey its secret to other men: all Blake's philosophy is but a desperate effort to persuade us to exchange the false world of "Nature" on which we usually look— and which is not really Nature at all—for this, the true world, to which he gave the confusing name of "Imagination." For these, the contemplation of the World of Becoming assumes the intense form which we call genius: even to read their poems is to feel the beating of a heart, the upleap of a joy, greater than anything that we have known. Yet your own little efforts towards the attainment of this level of consciousness will at least give to you, together with a more vivid universe, a wholly new comprehension of their works; and that of other poets and artists who have drunk from the chalice of the Spirit of Life. These works are now observed by you to be the only artistic creations to which the name of Realism is appropriate; and it is by the standard of reality that you shall now criticise them, recognising in utterances which you once dismissed as rhetoric the desperate efforts of the clear-sighted towards the exact description of things veritably seen in that simplified state of consciousness which Blake called "imagination uncorrupt."

It was from those purified and heightened levels of perception to which the first form of contemplation inducts the soul, that Julian of Norwich, gazing upon "a little thing, the quantity of an hazel nut," found in it the epitome of all that was made; for therein she perceived the royal character of life. So small and helpless in its mightiest forms, so august even in its meanest, that life in its wholeness was then realised by her as the direct outbirth of, and the meek dependant upon, the Energy of Divine Love. She felt at once the fugitive character of its apparent existence, the perdurable Reality within which it was held. "I marvelled," she said, "how it might last, for methought it might suddenly have fallen to naught for littleness. And I was answered in my understanding: *It lasteth, and ever shall, for that God loveth it.* And so All-thing hath the being by the love of God." To this same apprehension of Reality, this linking up of each finite expression with its Origin, this search for the inner significance of every fragment of life, one of the greatest and most balanced contemplatives of the nineteenth century, Florence Nightingale, reached out when she exclaimed in an hour of self-examination, "I must strive to see only God in my friends, and God in my cats."

Yet it is not the self-tormenting strife of intro-spective and self-conscious aspiration, but rather an unrelaxed, diligent intention, a steady acquies-cence, a simple and loyal surrender to the great currents of life, a holding on to results achieved in your best moments, that shall do it for you: a surrender not limp but deliberate, a trustful self-donation, a "living faith." "A pleasing stirring of love," says *The Cloud of Unknowing;* not a desperate anxious struggle for more light. True contemplation can only thrive when defended from two opposite exaggerations: quietism on the one hand, and spiritual fuss upon the other. Neither from passivity nor from anxiety has it anything to gain. Though the way may be long, the material of your mind intractable, to the eager lover of Reality ultimate success is assured. The strong tide of Transcendent Life will inevitably invade, clarify, uplift the consciousness which is open to receive it; a movement from without—subtle yet actual—answering each willed movement from within. "Your opening and His entering," says Eckhart, "are but one moment." When, therefore, you put aside your preconceived ideas, your self-centred scale of values, and let intuition have its way with you, you open up by this act new levels of the world. Such an opening-up is the most practical of all activities; for then and then only will your diurnal existence, and the natural scene in which that existence is set, begin to give up to you its richness and meaning. Its paradoxes and inequalities will be disclosed as true constituents of its beauty, an inconceivable splendour will be shaken out from its dingiest folds. Then, and only then, escaping the single vision of the selfish, you will

begin to guess all that your senses were meant to
be.

"I swear the earth shall surely be complete to him or her
who shall be complete,
The earth remains jagged and broken only to him or her
who remains jagged and broken."

CHAPTER VIII

THE SECOND FORM OF CONTEMPLATION

"AND here," says Ruysbroeck of the self which has reached this point, "there begins a hunger and a thirst which shall never more be stilled."

In the First Form of Contemplation that self has been striving to know better its own natural plane of existence. It has stretched out the feelers of its intuitive love into the general stream of duration of which it is a part. Breaking down the fences of personality, merging itself in a larger consciousness, it has learned to know the World of Becoming from within—as a citizen, a member of the great society of life, not merely as a spectator. But the more deeply and completely you become immersed in and aware of this life, the greater the extension of your consciousness; the more insistently will rumours and intimations of a higher plane of experience, a closer unity and more complete synthesis, begin to besiege you. You feel that hitherto you nave received the messages of life in a series of disconnected words and notes, from which your mind constructed as best it could certain coherent sentences and tunes—laws, classifications, relations, and the rest. But now you reach out towards the ultimate sentence and melody, which exist independently of your own constructive efforts; and realise that the words and notes which so often puzzled you by displaying an intensity that exceeded the demands of your little world, only have beauty and meaning just because and in so far as you discern them to be the partial expressions of a greater whole which is still beyond your reach.

You have long been like a child tearing up the petals of flowers in order to make a mosaic on the garden path; and the results of this murderous diligence you mistook for a knowledge of the world. When the bits fitted with unusual exactitude, you called it science. Now at last you have perceived the greater truth and loveliness of the living plant from which you broke them: have, in fact, entered into direct communion with it, "united" with its reality. But this very recognition of the living growing plant does and must entail for you a consciousness of deeper realities, which, as yet, you have not touched: of the intangible things and forces which feed and support it; of the whole universe that touches you through its life. A mere cataloguing of all the plants—though this were far better than your old game of indexing your own poor photographs of them—will never give you access to the Unity, the Fact, whatever it may be, which manifests itself through them. To suppose that it can do so is the cardinal error of the "nature mystic": an error parallel with that of the psychologist who looks for the soul in "psychic states."

The deeper your realisation of the plant in its wonder, the more perfect your union with the world of growth and change, the quicker, the more subtle your response to its countless suggestions; so much the more acute will become your craving for Something More. You will now find and feel the Infinite and Eternal, making as it were veiled and sacramental contacts with you under these accidents—through these its ceaseless crea-

tive activities—and you will want to press through
and beyond them, to a fuller realisation of, a
more perfect and unmediated union with, the
Substance of all That Is.   With the great widening and deepening of your life that has ensued
from the abolition of a narrow selfhood, your
entrance into the larger consciousness of living
things, there has necessarily come to you an in-
stinctive knowledge of a final and absolute group-
relation, transcending and including all lesser
unions in its sweep. To this, the second stage
of contemplation, in which human consciousness
enters into its peculiar heritage, something within
you now seems to urge you on.

If you obey this inward push, pressing forward
with the "sharp dart of your longing love," forcing
the point of your wilful attention further and
further into the web of things, such an ever-
deepening realisation, such an extension of your
conscious life, will indeed become possible to you.
Nothing but your own apathy, your feeble and
limited desire, limits this realisation.   Here there
is a strict relation between demand and supply—
your achievement shall be in proportion to the

greatness of your desire. The fact, and the in-pressing energy, of the Reality without does not vary. Only the extent to which you are able to receive it depends upon your courage and gener-osity, the measure in which you give yourself to its embrace. Those minds which set a limit to their self-donation must feel as they attain it, not a sense of satisfaction but a sense of constric-tion. It is useless to offer your spirit a garden— even a garden inhabited by saints and angels— and pretend that it has been made free of the universe. You will not have peace until you do away with all banks and hedges, and exchange the garden for the wilderness that is unwalled; that wild strange place of silence where "lovers lose themselves."

Yet you must begin this great adventure humbly; and take, as Julian of Norwich did, the first stage of your new outward-going journey along the road that lies nearest at hand. When Julian looked with the eye of contemplation upon that "little thing" which revealed to her the one-ness of the created universe, her deep and loving sight perceived in it successively three properties,

which she expressed as well as she might under
the symbols of her own theology: "The first is
that God made it; the second is that God loveth
it; the third is that God keepeth it." Here are
three phases in the ever-widening contemplative
apprehension of Reality. Not three opinions,
but three facts, for which she struggles to find
words. The first is that each separate living
thing, budding "like an hazel nut" upon the tree
of life, and there destined to mature, age, and
die, is the outbirth of another power, of a
creative push: that the World of Becoming in
all its richness and variety is not ultimate, but
formed by Something other than, and utterly
transcendent to, itself. This, of course, the
religious mind invariably takes for granted: but
we are concerned with immediate experience
rather than faith. To feel and know those two
aspects of Reality which we call "created" and
"uncreated," nature and spirit—to be as sharply
aware of them, as sure of them, as we are of land
and sea—is to be made free of the supersensual
world. It is to stand for an instant at the Poet's
side, and see that Poem of which you have de-

ciphered separate phrases in the earlier form of contemplation.   Then you were learning to read: and found in the words, the lines, the stanzas, an astonishing meaning and loveliness.   But how much greater the significance of every detail would appear to you, how much more truly you would possess its life, were you acquainted with the Poem: not as a mere succession of such lines and stanzas, but as a non-successional whole.

From this Julian passes to that deeper knowledge of the heart which comes from a humble and disinterested acceptance of life; that this Creation, this whole changeful natural order, with all its apparent collisions, cruelties, and waste, yet springs from an ardour, an immeasurable love, a perpetual donation, which generates it, upholds it, drives it; for "*all*-thing hath the being by the love of God."   Blake's anguished question here receives its answer: the Mind that conceived the lamb conceived the tiger too. Everything, says Julian in effect, whether gracious, terrible, or malignant, is enwrapped in love: and is part of a world produced, not by mechanical necessity, but by passionate desire.

Therefore nothing can really be mean, nothing despicable; nothing, however perverted, irredeemable. The blasphemous other-worldliness of the false mystic who conceives of matter as an evil thing and flies from its "deceits," is corrected by this loving sight. Hence, the more beautiful and noble a thing appears to us, the more we love it— so much the more truly do we see it: for then we perceive within it the Divine ardour surging up towards expression, and share that simplicity and purity of vision in which most saints and some poets see all things "as they are in God."

Lastly, this love-driven world of duration— this work within which the Divine Artist passionately and patiently expresses His infinite dream under finite forms—is held in another, mightier embrace. It is "kept," says Julian. Paradoxically, the perpetual changeful energies of love and creation which inspire it are gathered up and made complete within the unchanging fact of Being: the Eternal and Absolute, within which the world of things is set as the tree is set in the supporting earth, the enfolding air. There, finally, is the rock and refuge of the seeking consciousness wearied by the ceaseless process of the flux. There that flux exists in its wholeness, "all at once"; in a manner which we can never comprehend, but which in hours of withdrawal we may sometimes taste and feel. It is in man's moments of contact with this, when he penetrates beyond all images, however lovely, however significant, to that ineffable awareness which the mystics call "Naked Contemplation"—since it is stripped of all the clothing with which reason and imagination drape and disguise both our devils and our gods—that the hunger and thirst of the heart is satisfied, and we receive indeed an assurance of ultimate Reality. This assurance is not the cool conclusion of a successful argument. It is rather the seizing at last of Something which we have ever felt near us and enticing us: the unspeakably simple because completely inclusive solution of all the puzzles of life.

As, then, you gave yourself to the broken-up yet actual reality of the natural world, in order that it might give itself to you, and your possession of its secret was achieved, first by surrender of selfhood, next by a diligent thrusting

out of your attention, last by a union of love;
so now by a repetition upon fresh levels of that
same process, you are to mount up to higher unions
still.   Held tight as it seems to you in the finite,
committed to the perpetual rhythmic changes, the
unceasing flux of "natural" life—compelled to
pass on from state to state, to grow, to age, to
die—there is yet, as you discovered in the first
exercise of recollection, something in you which
endures through and therefore transcends this
world of change.   This inhabitant, this mobile
spirit, can spread and merge in the general consciousness, and gather itself again to one intense
point of personality.   It has too an innate
knowledge of—an instinct for—another, greater
rhythm, another order of Reality, as yet outside
its conscious field; or as we say, a capacity for
the Infinite.   This capacity, this unfulfilled craving, which the cunning mind of the practical man
suppresses and disguises as best it can, is the
source of all your unrest.   More, it is the true
origin of all your best loves and enthusiasms, the
inspiring cause of your heroisms and achieve-
ments; which are but oblique and tentative efforts

to still that strange hunger for some final object of devotion, some completing and elucidating vision, some total self-donation, some great and perfect Act within which your little activity can be merged.

St. Thomas Aquinas says, that a man is only withheld from this desired vision of the Divine Essence, this discovery of the Pure Act (which indeed is everywhere pressing in on him and supporting him), by the apparent necessity which he is under of turning to bodily images, of breaking up his continuous and living intuition into conceptual scraps; in other words, because he cannot live the life of sensation without thought. But it is not the man, it is merely his mental machinery which is under this "necessity." This it is which translates, analyses, incorporates in finite images the boundless perceptions of the spirit: passing through its prism the White Light of Reality, and shattering it to a succession of coloured rays. Therefore the man who would know the Divine Secret must unshackle himself more thoroughly than ever before from the tyranny of the image-making power. As it is

not by the methods of the laboratory that we learn
to know life, so it is not by the methods of the
intellect that we learn to know God.

"For of all other creatures and their works,"
says the author of *The Cloud of Unknowing*,
"yea, and of the works of God's self, may a man
through grace have full-head of knowing, and
well he can think of them: but of God Himself
can no man think.   And therefore I would leave
all that thing that I can think, and choose to
my love that thing that I cannot think.   For
why; He may well be loved, but not thought.
By love may He be gotten and holden; but by
thought never."

"Gotten and holden": homely words, that
suggest rather the outstretching of the hand to
take something lying at your very gates, than the
long outward journey or terrific ascent of the
contemplative soul.   Reality indeed, the mystics
say, is "near and far"; far from our thoughts,
but saturating and supporting our lives.   Nothing would be nearer, nothing dearer, nothing
sweeter, were the doors of our perception truly
cleansed.   You have then but to focus attention

upon your own deep reality, "realise your own soul," in order to find it. "We dwell in Him and He in us": you participate in the Eternal Order now. The vision of the Divine Essence —the participation of its own small activity in the Supernal Act—is for the spark of your soul a perpetual process. On the apex of your personality, spirit ever gazes upon Spirit, melts and merges in it: from and by this encounter its life arises and is sustained. But you have been busy from your childhood with other matters. All the urgent affairs of "life," as you absurdly called it, have monopolised your field of consciousness. Thus all the important events of your real life, physical and spiritual—the mysterious perpetual growth of you, the knitting up of fresh bits of the universe into the unstable body which you confuse with yourself, the hum and whirr of the machine which preserves your contacts with the material world, the more delicate movements which condition your correspondences with, and growth within, the spiritual order—all these have gone on unperceived by you. All the time you have been kept and nourished, like the "Little Thing," by an enfolding and creative love; yet of this you are less conscious than you are of the air that you breathe.

Now, as in the first stage of contemplation you learned and established, as a patent and experienced fact, your fraternal relation with all the other children of God, entering into the rhythm of their existence, participating in their stress and their joy; will you not at least try to make patent this your filial relation too? This actualisation of your true status, your place in the Eternal World, is waiting for you. It represents the next phase in your gradual achievement of Reality. The method by which you will attain to it is strictly analogous to that by which you obtained a more vivid awareness of the natural world in which you grow and move. Here too it shall be direct intuitive contact, sensation rather than thought, which shall bring you certitude—"tasting food, not talking about it," as St. Bonaventura says.

Yet there is a marked difference between these two stages. In the first, the deliberate inward retreat and gathering together of your faculties which was effected by recollection, was the prelude

to a new coming forth, an outflow from the
narrow limits of a merely personal life to the
better and truer apprehension of the created
world.   Now, in the second stage, the disciplined
and recollected attention seems to take an opposite
course.   It is directed towards a plane of existence with which your bodily senses have no
attachments: which is not merely misrepresented
by your ordinary concepts, but cannot be represented by them at all.   It must therefore sink
inwards towards its own centre, "away from all
that can be thought or felt," as the mystics say,
"away from every image, every notion, every
thing," towards that strange condition of obscurity which St. John of the Cross calls the "Night
of Sense."   Do this steadily, checking each
vagrant instinct, each insistent thought, however
"spiritual" it may seem; pressing ever more deeply
inwards towards that ground, that simple and
undifferentiated Being from which your diverse
faculties emerge.   Presently you will find yourself, emptied and freed, in a place stripped bare
of all the machinery of thought; and achieve the
condition of simplicity which those same special-

ists call nakedness of spirit or "Wayless Love,"
and which they declare to be above all human
images and ideas—a state of consciousness in
which "all the workings of the reason fail."
Then you will observe that you have entered into
an intense and vivid silence: a silence which exists in itself, through and in spite of the ceaseless noises of your normal world. Within this
world of silence you seem as it were to lose yourself, "to ebb and to flow, to wander and be lost
in the Imageless Ground," says Ruysbroeck,
struggling to describe the sensations of the self
in this, its first initiation into the "wayless world,
beyond image," where "all is, yet in no wise."

Yet in spite of the darkness that enfolds you,
the Cloud of Unknowing into which you have
plunged, you are sure that it is well to be here.
A peculiar certitude which you cannot analyse,
a strange satisfaction and peace, is distilled into
you. You begin to understand what the Psalm-
ist meant, when he said, "Be still, and know."
You are lost in a wilderness, a solitude, a dim
strange state of which you can say nothing, since
it offers no material to your image-making mind.

But this wilderness, from one point of view so bare and desolate, from another is yet strangely homely. In it, all your sorrowful questionings are answered without utterance; it is the All, and you are within it and part of it, and know that it is good. It calls forth the utmost adoration of which you are capable; and, mysteriously, gives love for love. You have ascended now, say the mystics, into the Freedom of the Will of God; are become part of a higher, slower duration, which carries you as it were upon its bosom and —though never perhaps before has your soul been so truly active—seems to you a stillness, a rest.

The doctrine of Plotinus concerning a higher life of unity, a lower life of multiplicity, possible to every human spirit, will now appear to you not a fantastic theory, but a plain statement of fact, which you have verified in your own experience. You perceive that these are the two complementary ways of apprehending and uniting with Reality—the one as a dynamic process, the other as an eternal whole. Thus understood, they do not conflict. You know that the flow, the broken-up world of change and multiplicity, is still going on; and that you, as a creature of the time-world, are moving and growing with it. But, thanks to the development of the higher side of your consciousness, you are now lifted to a new poise; a direct participation in that simple, transcendent life "broken, yet not divided," which gives to this time-world all its meaning and validity. And you know, without derogation from the realness of that life of flux within which you first made good your attachments to the universe, that you are also a true constituent of the greater whole; that since you are man, you are also spirit, and are living Eternal Life now, in the midst of time.

The effect of this form of contemplation, in the degree in which the ordinary man may learn to practise it, is like the sudden change of atmosphere, the shifting of values, which we experience when we pass from the busy streets into a quiet church; where a lamp burns, and a silence reigns, the same yesterday, to-day, and for ever. Thence is poured forth a stillness which strikes through the tumult without. Eluding the flicker of the arc-lamps, thence through an upper window we may glimpse a perpetual star.

The walls of the church, limiting the range of our attention, shutting out the torrent of life, with its insistent demands and appeals, make possible our apprehension of this deep eternal peace. The character of our consciousness, intermediate between Eternity and Time, and ever ready to swing between them, makes such a device, such a concrete aid to concentration, essential to us. But the peace, the presence, is everywhere—for us, not for it, is the altar and the sanctuary required—and your deliberate, humble practice of contemplation will teach you at last to find it; outside the sheltering walls of recollection as well as within. You will realise then what Julian meant, when she declared the ultimate property of all that was made to be that "God keepeth it": will *feel* the violent consciousness of an enfolding Presence, utterly transcending the fluid changeful nature-life, and incomprehensible to the intelligence which that nature-life has developed and trained. And as you knew the secret of that nature-life best by surrendering yourself to it, by entering its currents, and refusing to analyse or arrange: so here, by a deliberate giving of yourself to the silence, the rich "nothingness," the "Cloud," you will draw nearest to the Reality it conceals from the eye of sense. "Lovers put out the candle and draw the curtains," says Patmore, "when they wish to see the God and the Goddess: and in the higher communion, the night of thought is the light of perception."

Such an experience of Eternity, the attainment of that intuitive awareness, that meek and simple self-mergence, which the mystics call sometimes, according to its degree and special circumstances, the Quiet, the Desert of God, the Divine Dark, represents the utmost that human consciousness can do of itself towards the achievement of union with Reality. To some it brings joy and peace, to others fear: to all a paradoxical sense of the lowliness and greatness of the soul, which now at last can measure itself by the august standards of the Infinite. Though the trained and diligent will of the contemplative can, if control of the attention be really established, recapture this state of awareness, retreat into the Quiet again and again, yet it is of necessity a fleeting experience; for man is immersed in duration, subject to it. Its demands upon his attention can only cease with the cessation of physical life—perhaps not then. Perpetual absorption in the Transcendent is a human impossibility, and the effort to achieve it is both unsocial and silly. But this experience, this "ascent to the Nought," changes for ever the proportions of the life that once has known it; gives to it depth and height, and prepares the way for those further experiences, that great transfiguration of existence which comes when the personal activity of the finite will gives place to the great and compelling action of another Power.

CHAPTER IX

THE THIRD FORM OF CONTEMPLATION

THE hard separation which some mystical writers insist upon making between "natural" and "supernatural" contemplation, has been on the whole productive of confusion rather than clearness: for the word "supernatural" has many unfortunate associations for the mind of the plain man. It at once suggests to him visions and ecstasies, superstitious beliefs, ghosts, and other disagreeable interferences with the order which he calls "natural"; and inclines him to his old attitude of suspicion in respect of all mystical things. But some word we must have, to indicate the real cleavage which exists between the second and third stages in the development of the contemplative consciousness: the real change which, if you would go further on these interior paths, must now take place in the manner of your apprehension of Reality. Hitherto, all that you have at-

tained has been—or at least has seemed to you—
the direct result of your own hard work.   A difficult self-discipline, the slowly achieved control of
your vagrant thoughts and desires, the steady
daily practice of recollection, a diligent pushing
out of your consciousness from the superficial to
the fundamental, an unselfish loving attention;
all this has been rewarded by the gradual broaden-
ing and deepening of your perceptions, by an
initiation into the movements of a larger life.
You have been a knocker, a seeker, an asker: have
beat upon the Cloud of Unknowing "with a sharp
dart of longing love."   A perpetual effort of the
will has characterised your inner development.
Your contemplation, in fact, as the specialists
would say, has been "active," not "infused."

But now, having achieved an awareness—obscure and indescribable indeed, yet actual—of the
enfolding presence of Reality, under those two
forms which the theologians call the "immanence"
and the "transcendence" of the Divine, a change
is to take place in the relation between your finite
human spirit and the Infinite Life in which at
last it knows itself to dwell.   All that will now

come to you—and much perhaps will come—will happen as it seems without effort on your own part: though really it will be the direct result of that long stress and discipline which has gone before, and has made it possible for you to feel the subtle contact of deeper realities. It will depend also on the steady continuance—often perhaps through long periods of darkness and boredom—of that poise to which you have been trained: the stretching-out of the loving and surrendered will into the dimness and silence, the continued trustful habitation of the soul in the atmosphere of the Essential World. You are like a traveller arrived in a new country. The journey has been a long one; and the hardships and obstacles involved in it, the effort, the perpetual conscious pressing forward, have at last come to seem the chief features of your inner life. Now, with their cessation, you feel curiously lost; as if the chief object of your existence had been taken away. No need to push on any further: yet, though there is no more that you can do of yourself, there is much that may and must be done to you. The place that you have come to seems strange and

bewildering, for it lies far beyond the horizons
of human thought.   There are no familiar land-
marks, nothing on which you can lay hold.   You
"wander to and fro," as the mystics say, "in this
fathomless ground"; surrounded by silence and
darkness, struggling to breathe this rarefied air.
Like those who go to live in new latitudes, you
must become acclimatised.   Your state, then,
should now be wisely passive; in order that the
great influences which surround you may take
and adjust your spirit, that the unaccustomed
light, which now seems to you a darkness, may
clarify your eyes, and that you may be trans-
formed from a visitor into an inhabitant of that
supernal Country which St. Augustine described
as "no mere vision, but a home."

You are therefore to let yourself go; to cease
all conscious, anxious striving and pushing.
Finding yourself in this place of darkness and
quietude, this "Night of the Spirit," as St. John
of the Cross has called it, you are to dwell there
meekly; asking nothing, seeking nothing, but with
your doors flung wide open towards God.   And
as you do thus, there will come to you an ever

clearer certitude that this darkness enveils the
goal for which you have been seeking from the
first; the final Reality with which you are destined
to unite, the perfect satisfaction of your most ardent and most sacred desires.   It is there, but you
cannot by your efforts reach it.   This realisation
of your own complete impotence, of the resistance
which the Transcendent—long sought and faith-
fully served—now seems to offer to your busy
outgoing will and love, your ardour, your deliberate self-donation, is at once the most painful and
most essential phase in the training of the human
soul.   It brings you into that state of passive
suffering which is to complete the decentralisa-
tion of your character, test the purity of your love,
and perfect your education in humility.

Here, you must oppose more thoroughly than
ever before the instincts and suggestions of your
separate, clever, energetic self; which, hating
silence and dimness, is always trying to take the
methods of Martha into the domain of Mary,
and seldom discriminates between passivity and
sloth.   Perhaps you will find, when you try to
achieve this perfect self-abandonment, that a

further, more drastic self-exploration, a deeper, more searching purification than that which was forced upon you by your first experience of the recollective state is needed. The last fragments of selfhood, the very desire for spiritual satisfaction—the fundamental human tendency to drag down the Simple Fact and make it ours, instead of offering ourselves to it—must be sought out and killed. In this deep contemplation, this profound Quiet, your soul gradually becomes conscious of a constriction, a dreadful narrowness of personality; something still existing in itself, still tending to draw inwards to its own centre, and keeping it from that absolute surrender which is the only way to peace. An attitude of perfect generosity, complete submission, willing acquiescence in anything that may happen—even in failure and death—is here your only hope: for union with Reality can only be a union of love, a glad and humble self-mergence in the universal life. You must, so far as you are able, give yourself up to, "die into," melt into the Whole; abandon all efforts to lay hold of It. More, you must be willing that it should lay hold of you. "A pure

bare going forth," says Tauler, trying to describe
the sensations of the self at this moment.
"None," says Ruysbroeck, putting this same experience, this meek outstreaming of the bewildered
spirit, into other language, "is sure of Eternal
Life, unless he has died with his own attributes
wholly into God."

It is unlikely that agreeable emotions will ac-
company this utter self-surrender; for everything
will now seem to be taken from you, nothing given
in exchange. But if you are able to make it, a
mighty transformation will result. From the
transitional plane of darkness, you will be re-
born into another "world," another stage of realisation: and find yourself, literally, to be other
than you were before. Ascetic writers tell us that
the essence of the change now effected consists in
the fact that "God's *action* takes the place of
man's *activity*"—that the surrendered self "does
not act, but receives." By this they mean to describe, as well as our concrete language will permit, the new and vivid consciousness which now
invades the contemplative; the sense which he has
of being as it were helpless in the grasp of another

Power, so utterly part of him, so completely different from him—so rich and various, so transfused with life and feeling, so urgent and so all-transcending—that he can only think of it as God.   It is for this that the dimness and steadily increasing passivity of the stage of Quiet has been preparing him; and it is out of this willing quietude and ever-deepening obscurity that the new experiences come.

> "O night that didst lead thus,
> O night more lovely than the dawn of light,
> O night that broughtest us
> Lover to lover's sight—
> Lover with loved in marriage of delight,"

says St. John of the Cross in the most wonderful of all mystical poems.   "He who has had experience of this," says St. Teresa of the same stage of apprehension, "will understand it in some measure: but it cannot be more clearly described because what then takes place is so obscure.   All I am able to say is, that the soul is represented as being close to God; and that there abide a conviction thereof so certain and strong, that it cannot possibly help believing so."

This sense, this conviction, which may be translated by the imagination into many different forms, is the substance of the greatest experiences and highest joys of the mystical saints. The intensity with which it is realised will depend upon the ardour, purity, and humility of the experiencing soul: but even those who feel it faintly are convinced by it for evermore. In some great and generous spirits, able to endure the terrific onslaught of Reality, it may even reach a vividness by which all other things are obliterated; and the self, utterly helpless under the inundations of this transcendent life-force, passes into that simple state of consciousness which is called Ecstasy.

But you are not to be frightened by these special manifestations; or to suppose that here the road is barred against you. Though these great spirits have as it were a genius for Reality, a susceptibility to supernal impressions, so far beyond your own small talent that there seems no link between you: yet you have, since you are human, a capacity for the Infinite too. With less intensity, less splendour, but with a certitude which no arguments will ever shake, this sense of the Living

Fact, and of its mysterious contacts with and invasions of the human spirit, may assuredly be realised by you. This realisation—sometimes felt under the symbols of personality, sometimes under those of an impersonal but life-giving Force, Light, Energy, or Heat—is the ruling character of the third phase of contemplation; and the reward of that meek passivity, that "busy idleness" as the mystics sometimes call it, which you have been striving to attain. Sooner or later, if you are patient, it will come to you through the darkness: a mysterious contact, a clear certitude of intercourse and of possession—perhaps so gradual in its approach that the break, the change from the ever-deepening stillness and peace of the second phase, is hardly felt by you; perhaps, if your nature be ardent and unstable, with a sudden shattering violence, in a "storm of love."

In either case, the advent of this experience is incalculable, and completely outside your own control. So far, to use St. Teresa's well-known image, you have been watering the garden of your spirit by hand; a poor and laborious method, yet one in which there is a definite relation between effort and result. But now the watering-can is taken from you, and you must depend upon the rain: more generous, more fruitful, than anything which your own efforts could manage, but, in its incalculable visitations, utterly beyond your control. Here all one can say is this: that if you acquiesce in the heroic demands which the spiritual life now makes upon you, if you let yourself go, eradicate the last traces of self-interest even of the most spiritual kind—then, you have established conditions under which the forces of the spiritual world can work on you, heightening your susceptibilities, deepening and purifying your attention, so that you are able to taste and feel more and more of the inexhaustible riches of Reality.

Thus dying to your own will, waiting for what is given, infused, you will presently find that a change in your apprehension has indeed taken place: and that those who said self-loss was the only way to realisation taught no pious fiction but the truth. The highest contemplative experience to which you have yet attained has seemed above all else a still awareness. The cessation of your own striving, a resting upon and within the Absolute World—these were its main characteristics for your consciousness. But now, this Ocean of Being is no longer felt by you as an emptiness, a solitude without bourne. Suddenly you know it to be instinct with a movement and life too great for you to apprehend. You are thrilled by a mighty energy, uncontrolled by you, unsolicited by you: its higher vitality is poured into your soul. You enter upon an experience for which all the terms of power, thought, motion, even of love, are inadequate: yet which contains within itself the only complete expression of all these things. Your strength is now literally made perfect in weakness: because of the completeness of your dependence, a fresh life is infused into you, such as your old separate existence never knew. Moreover, to that diffused and impersonal sense of the Infinite, in which you have dipped yourself, and which swallows up and completes all the ideas your mind has ever built up with the help of the categories of time and space, is now added the consciousness of a Living Fact which includes, transcends, completes all that you mean by the categories of personality and of life. Those ineffective, half-conscious attempts towards free action, clear apprehension, true union, which we dignify by the names of will, thought, and love are now seen matched by an Absolute Will, Thought, and Love; instantly recognised by the contemplating spirit as the highest reality it yet has known, and evoking in it a passionate and a humble joy.

This unmistakable experience has been achieved by the mystics of every religion; and when we read their statements, we know that all are speaking of the same thing. None who have had it have ever been able to doubt its validity. It has always become for them the central fact, by which all other realities must be tested and graduated. It has brought to them the deep consciousness of sources of abundant life now made accessible to man; of the impact of a mighty energy, gentle, passionate, self-giving, creative, which they can only call Absolute Love. Sometimes they feel this strange life moving and stirring within them. Sometimes it seems to pursue, entice, and besiege them. In every case, they are the passive objects upon which it works. It is now another Power which seeks the separated spirit and demands it; which knocks at the closed door of the narrow personality; which penetrates the contemplative consciousness through and through, speaking, stirring, compelling it; which sometimes, by its secret irresistible pressure, wins even the most recalcitrant in spite of themselves. Sometimes this Power is felt as an impersonal force, the unifying cosmic energy, the indrawing love which gathers all things into One; sometimes as a sudden access of vitality, a light and heat, enfolding and penetrating the self and making its languid life more vivid and more real; sometimes as a personal and friendly Presence which counsels and entreats the soul.

In each case, the mystics insist again that this is God; that here under these diverse manners the soul has immediate intercourse with Him. But we must remember that when they make this declaration, they are speaking from a plane of consciousness far above the ideas and images of popular religion; and from a place which is beyond the judiciously adjusted horizon of philosophy. They mean by this word, not a notion, however august; but an experienced Fact so vivid, that against it the so-called facts of daily life look shadowy and insecure. They say that this Fact is "immanent"; dwelling in, transfusing, and discoverable through every aspect of the universe, every movement of the game of life—as you have found in the first stage of contemplation. There you may hear its melody and discern its form. And further, that It is "transcendent"; in essence exceeding and including the sum of those glimpses and contacts which we obtain by self-mergence in life, and in Its simplest manifestations above and beyond anything to which reason can attain—"the Nameless Being, of Whom nought can be said." This you discovered to be true in the second stage. But in addition to this, they say also, that this all-pervasive, all-changing, and yet changeless One, Whose melody is heard in all movement, and within Whose Being "the worlds are being told like beads," calls the human spirit to an immediate intercourse, a *unity*, a fruition, a divine give-and-take, for which the contradictory symbols of feeding, of touching, of marriage, of immersion, are all too poor; and which evokes in the fully conscious soul a passionate and a humble love. "He devours us and He feeds us!" exclaims Ruysbroeck. "Here," says St. Thomas Aquinas, "the soul in a wonderful and unspeakable manner both seizes and is seized upon, devours and is herself devoured, embraces and is violently embraced: and by the knot of love she unites herself with God, and is with Him as the Alone with the Alone."

The marvellous love-poetry of mysticism, the rhapsodies which extol the spirit's Lover, Friend, Companion, Bridegroom; which describe the "deliberate speed, majestic instancy" of the Hound of Heaven chasing the separated soul, the onslaughts, demands, and caresses of this "stormy, generous, and unfathomable love"—all this is an attempt, often of course oblique and symbolic in method, to express and impart this transcendent secret, to describe that intense yet elusive state in which alone union with the living heart of Reality is possible. "How delicately Thou teachest love to me!" cries St. John of the Cross; and here indeed we find all the ardours of all earthly lovers justified by an imperishable Objective, which re-

veals Itself in all things that we truly love, and
beyond all these things both seeks us and compels
us, "giving more than we can take and asking
more than we can pay."

You do not, you never will know, *what* this
Objective is: for as Dionysius teaches, "if any
one saw God and understood what he saw, then
it was not God that he saw, but something that
belongs to Him." But you do know now that it
exists, with an intensity which makes all other
existences unreal; save in so far as they participate
in this one Fact. "Some contemplate the Form-
less, and others meditate on Form: but the wise
man knows that Brahma is beyond both." As
you yield yourself more and more completely to
the impulses of this intimate yet unseizable Presence, so much the sweeter and stronger—so much
the more constant and steady—will your intercourse with it become. The imperfect music of
your adoration will be answered and reinforced
by another music, gentle, deep, and strange; your
out-going movement, the stretching forth of your
desire from yourself to something other, will be
answered by a movement, a stirring, within you

yet not conditioned by you. The wonder and variety of this intercourse is never-ending. It includes in its sweep every phase of human love and self-devotion, all beauty and all power, all suffering and effort, all gentleness and rapture: here found in synthesis. Going forth into the bareness and darkness of this unwalled world of high contemplation, you there find stored for you, and at last made real, all the highest values, all the dearest and noblest experiences of the world of growth and change.

You see now what it is that you have been doing in the course of your mystical development. As your narrow heart stretched to a wider sympathy with life, you have been surrendering progressively to larger and larger existences, more and more complete realities: have been learning to know them, to share their very being, through the magic of disinterested love. First, the manifested, flowing, evolving life of multiplicity: felt by you in its wonder and wholeness, once you learned to yield yourself to its rhythms, received in simplicity the undistorted messages of sense. Then, the actual unchanging ground of life, the

eternal and unconditioned Whole, transcending all
succession: a world inaccessible alike to senses
and intelligence, but felt—vaguely, darkly, yet
intensely—by the quiet and surrendered consciousness. But now you are solicited, whether
you will or no, by a greater Reality, the final inclusive Fact, the Unmeasured Love, which "is
through all things everlastingly": and yielding
yourself to it, receiving and responding to its
obscure yet ardent communications, you pass beyond the cosmic experience to the personal encounter, the simple yet utterly inexpressible union
of the soul with its God.

And this threefold union with Reality, as your
attention is focussed now on one aspect, now on
another, of its rich simplicity, will be actualised
by you in many different ways: for you are not to
suppose that an unchanging barren ecstasy is now
to characterise your inner life. Though the sense
of your own dwelling within the Eternal transfuses
and illuminates it, the sense of your own necessary
efforts, a perpetual renewal of contact with the
Spiritual World, a perpetual self-donation, shall
animate it too. When the greater love over-

whelms the lesser, and your small self-conscious-
ness is lost in the consciousness of the Whole, it
will be felt as an intense stillness, a quiet fruition
of Reality. Then, your very selfhood seems to
cease, as it does in all your moments of great
passion; and you are "satisfied and overflowing,
and with Him beyond yourself eternally ful-
filled." Again, when your own necessary activity
comes into the foreground, your small energetic
love perpetually pressing to deeper and deeper
realisation—"tasting through and through, and
seeking through and through, the fathomless
ground" of the Infinite and Eternal—it seems
rather a perpetually renewed encounter than a
final achievement. Since you are a child of Time
as well as of Eternity, such effort and satisfaction,
active and passive love are both needed by you, if
your whole life is to be brought into union with
the inconceivably rich yet simple One in Whom
these apparent opposites are harmonised. Therefore seeking and finding, work and rest, conflict
and peace, feeding on God and self-immersion in
God, spiritual marriage and spiritual death—these
contradictory images are all wanted, if we are to

represent the changing moods of the living, grow-ing human spirit; the diverse aspects under which it realises the simple fact of its intercourse with the Divine.

Each new stage achieved in the mystical de-velopment of the spirit has meant, not the leaving behind of the previous stages, but an adding on to them: an ever greater extension of experience, and enrichment of personality. So that the total result of this change, this steady growth of your transcendental self, is not an impoverishment of the sense-life in the supposed interests of the super-sensual, but the addition to it of another life—a huge widening and deepening of the field over which your attention can play. Sometimes the mature contemplative consciousness narrows to an intense point of feeling, in which it seems indeed "alone with the Alone": sometimes it spreads to a vast apprehension of the Universal Life, or per-ceives the common things of sense aflame with God. It moves easily and with no sense of in-congruity from hours of close personal commun-ion with its Friend and Lover to self-loss in the "deep yet dazzling darkness" of the Divine

Abyss: or, re-entering that living world of change which the first form of contemplation disclosed to it, passes beyond those discrete manifestations of Reality to realise the Whole which dwells in and inspires every part. Thus ascending to the mysterious fruition of that Reality which is beyond image, and descending again to the loving contemplation and service of all struggling growing things, it now finds and adores everywhere—in the sky and the nest, the soul and the void—one Energetic Love which "is measureless, since it is all that exists," and of which the patient upclimb of the individual soul, the passionate outpouring of the Divine Mind, form the completing opposites.

CHAPTER X

THE MYSTICAL LIFE

AND here the practical man, who has been strangely silent during the last stages of our discourse, shakes himself like a terrier which has achieved dry land again after a bath; and asks once more, with a certain explosive violence, his dear old question, "What is the *use* of all this?"

"You have introduced me," he says further, "to some curious states of consciousness, interesting enough in their way; and to a lot of peculiar emotions, many of which are no doubt most valuable to poets and so on. But it is all so remote from daily life. How is it going to fit in with ordinary existence? How, above all, is it all going to help *me?*"

Well, put upon its lowest plane, this new way of attending to life—this deepening and widening of outlook—may at least be as helpful to you as

148

many things to which you have unhesitatingly
consecrated much time and diligence in the past:
your long journeys to new countries, for instance,
or long hours spent in acquiring new "facts," re-
labelling old experiences, gaining skill in new arts
and games. These, it is true, were quite worth
the effort expended on them: for they gave you,
in exchange for your labour and attention, a fresh
view of certain fragmentary things, a new point
of contact with the rich world of possibilities, a
tiny enlargement of your universe in one direction or another. Your love and patient study of
nature, art, science, politics, business—even of
sport—repaid you thus. But I have offered you,
in exchange for a meek and industrious attention
to another aspect of the world, hitherto somewhat
neglected by you, an enlargement which shall include and transcend all these; and be conditioned
only by the perfection of your generosity, courage, and surrender.

Nor are you to suppose that this enlargement
will be limited to certain new spiritual perceptions,
which the art of contemplation has made possible for you: that it will merely draw the curtain

from a window out of which you have never looked. This new wide world is not to be for you something seen, but something lived in: and you—since man is a creature of responses—will insensibly change under its influence, growing up into a more perfect conformity with it. Living in this atmosphere of Reality, you will, in fact, yourself become more real. Hence, if you accept in a spirit of trust the suggestions which have been made to you—and I acknowledge that here at the beginning an attitude of faith is essential—and if you practise with diligence the arts which I have described: then, sooner or later, you will inevitably find yourself deeply and permanently changed by them—will perceive that you have become a "new man." Not merely have you acquired new powers of perception and new ideas of Reality; but a quiet and complete transformation, a strengthening and maturing of your personality has taken place.

You are still, it is true, living the ordinary life of the body. You are immersed in the stream of duration; a part of the human, the social, the national group. The emotions, instincts, needs,

of that group affect you.   Your changing scrap of
vitality contributes to its corporate life; and contributes the more effectively since a new, intuitive
sympathy has now made its interests your own.
Because of that corporate life, transfusing you,
giving to you and taking from you—conditioning
you as it does in countless oblique and unapparent
ways—you are still compelled to react to many
suggestions which you are no longer able to respect: controlled, to the last moment of your
bodily existence and perhaps afterwards, by habit,
custom, the good old average way of misunder-
standing the world.   To this extent, the crowd-
spirit has you in its grasp.

Yet in spite of all this, you are now released
from that crowd's tyrannically overwhelming consciousness as you never were before.   You feel
yourself now a separate vivid entity, a real, whole
man: dependent on the Whole, and gladly so
dependent, yet within that Whole a free self-gov-
erning thing.   Perhaps you always fancied that
your will was free—that you were actually, as
you sometimes said, the "captain of your soul."
If so, this was merely one amongst the many illu-

sions which supported your old, enslaved career. As a matter of fact, you were driven along a road, unaware of anything that lay beyond the hedges, pressed on every side by other members of the flock; getting perhaps a certain satisfaction out of the deep warm stir of the collective life, but ignorant of your destination, and with your personal initiative limited to the snatching of grass as you went along, the pushing of your way to the softer side of the track. These operations made up together that which you called Success. But now, because you have achieved a certain power of gathering yourself together, perceiving yourself as a person, a spirit, and observing your relation with these other individual lives—because too, hearing now and again the mysterious piping of the Shepherd, you realise your own perpetual forward movement and that of the flock, in its relation to that living guide—you have a far deeper, truer knowledge than ever before both of the general and the individual existence; and so are able to handle life with a surer hand.

Do not suppose from this that your new career is to be perpetually supported by agreeable spirit-

ual contacts, or occupy itself in the mild contemplation of the great world through which you
move. True, it is said of the Shepherd that he
carries the lambs in his bosom: but the sheep are
expected to walk, and put up with the inequalities of the road, the bunts and blunders of the
flock. It is to vigour rather than to comfort that
you are called. Since the transcendental aspect
of your being has been brought into focus you
are now raised out of the mere push-forward, the
blind passage through time of the flock, into a
position of creative responsibility. You are
aware of personal correspondences with the
Shepherd. You correspond, too, with a larger,
deeper, broader world. The sky and the hedges,
the wide lands through which you are moving, the
corporate character and meaning of the group to
which you belong—all these are now within the
circle of your consciousness; and each little event,
each separate demand or invitation which comes
to you is now seen in a truer proportion, because
you bring to it your awareness of the Whole.
Your journey ceases to be an automatic progress,
and takes on some of the characters of a free act:

for "things" are now under you, you are no longer under them.

You will hardly deny that this is a practical gain: that this widening and deepening of the range over which your powers of perception work makes you more of a man than you were before, and thus adds to rather than subtracts from your total practical efficiency. It is indeed only when he reaches these levels, and feels within himself this creative freedom—this full actualisation of himself—on the one hand: on the other hand the sense of a world-order, a love and energy on which he depends and with whose interests he is now at one, that man becomes fully human, capable of living the real life of Eternity in the midst of the world of time.

And what, when you have come to it, do you suppose to be your own function in this vast twofold scheme? Is it for nothing, do you think, that you are thus a meeting-place of two orders? Surely it is your business, so far as you may, to express in action something of the real character of that universe within which you now know yourself to live? Artists, aware of a more vivid and more beautiful world than other men, are always driven by their love and enthusiasm to try and express, bring into direct manifestation, those deeper significances of form, sound, rhythm, which they have been able to apprehend: and, doing this, they taste deeper and deeper truths, make ever closer unions with the Real. For them, the duty of creation is tightly bound up with the gift of love. In their passionate outflowing to the universe which offers itself under one of its many aspects to their adoration, that other-worldly fruition of beauty is always followed, balanced, completed, by a this-world impulse to creation: a desire to fix within the time-order, and share with other men, the vision by which they were possessed. Each one, thus bringing new aspects of beauty, new ways of seeing and hearing within the reach of the race, does something to amend the sorry universe of common sense, the more hideous universe of greed, and redeem his fellows from their old, slack servitude to a lower range of significances. It is in action, then, that these find their truest and safest point of insertion into the living, active world of Reality: in sharing and furthering its work of manifestation they know its secrets best. For them contemplation and action are not opposites, but two interdependent forms of a life that is *one*—a life that rushes out to a passionate communion with the true and beautiful, only that it may draw from this direct experience of Reality a new intensity wherewith to handle the world of things; and remake it, or at least some little bit of it, "nearer to the heart's desire."

Again, the great mystics tell us that the "vision of God in His own light"—the direct contact of the soul's substance with the Absolute—to which awful experience you drew as near as the quality of your spirit would permit in the third degree of contemplation, is the prelude, not to a further revelation of the eternal order given to you, but to an utter change, a vivid life springing up within you, which they sometimes call the "transforming union" or the "birth of the Son in the soul." By this they mean that the spark of spiritual stuff, that high special power or character of human nature, by which you first desired, then tended to, then achieved contact with Reality, is as it were fertilised by this profound communion with its origin; becomes strong and vigorous, invades and transmutes the whole personality, and makes of it, not a "dreamy mystic" but an active and impassioned servant of the Eternal Wisdom.

So that when these full-grown, fully vital mystics try to tell us about the life they have achieved, it is always an intensely active life that they describe. They say, not that they "dwell in restful fruition," though the deep and joyous knowledge of this, perhaps too the perpetual longing for an utter self-loss in it, is always possessed by them —but that they "go up *and down* the ladder of contemplation." They stretch up towards the Point, the unique Reality to which all the intricate and many-coloured lines of life flow, and in which they are merged; and rush out towards those various lives in a passion of active love and service. This double activity, this swinging between rest and work—this alone, they say, is truly the life of man; because this alone represents on human levels something of that inexhaustibly rich yet simple life, "ever active yet ever at rest," which they find in God. When he gets to this, then man has indeed actualised his union with

Reality; because then he is a part of the perpetual creative act, the eternal generation of the Divine thought and love. Therefore contemplation, even at its highest, dearest, and most intimate, is not to be for you an end in itself. It shall only be truly yours when it impels you to action: when the double movement of Transcendent Love, drawing inwards to unity and fruition, and rushing out again to creative acts, is realised in you. You are to be a living, ardent tool with which the Supreme Artist works: one of the instruments of His self-manifestation, the perpetual process by which His Reality is brought into concrete expression.

Now the expression of vision, of reality, of beauty, at an artist's hands—the creation of new life in all forms—has two factors: the living moulding creative spirit, and the material in which it works. Between these two there is inevitably a difference of tension. The material is at best inert, and merely patient of the informing idea; at worst, directly recalcitrant to it. Hence, according to the balance of these two factors, the amount of resistance offered by stuff to tool, a greater or less energy must be expended, greater or less perfection of result will be achieved. You, accepting the wide deep universe of the mystic, and the responsibilities that go with it, have by this act taken sides once for all with creative spirit: with the higher tension, the unrelaxed effort, the passion for a better, intenser, and more significant life. The adoration to which you are vowed is not an affair of red hassocks and authorised hymn books; but a burning and consuming fire. You will find, then, that the world, going its own gait, busily occupied with its own system of correspondences—yielding to every gust of passion, intent on the satisfaction of greed, the struggle for comfort or for power—will oppose your new eagerness; perhaps with violence, but more probably with the exasperating calmness of a heavy animal which refuses to get up. If your new life is worth anything, it will flame to sharper power when it strikes against this dogged inertness of things: for you need resistances on which to act. "The road to a Yea lies through a Nay," and righteous warfare is the only way to a living and a lasting peace.

Further, you will observe more and more clearly, that the stuff of your external world, the method and machinery of the common life, is not merely passively but actively inconsistent with your sharp interior vision of truth. The heavy animal is diseased as well as indolent. All man's perverse ways of seeing his universe, all the perverse and hideous acts which have sprung from them—these have set up reactions, have produced deep disorders in the world of things. Man is free, and holds the keys of hell as well as the keys of heaven. Within the love-driven universe which you have learned to see as a whole, you will therefore find egotism, rebellion, meanness, brutality, squalor: the work of separated selves whose energies are set athwart the stream. But every aspect of life, however falsely imagined, can still be "saved," turned to the purposes of Reality: for "all-thing hath the being by the love of God." Its oppositions are no part of its realness; and therefore they can be overcome. Is there not here, then, abundance of practical work for you to do; work which is the direct outcome of your mystical experience? Are there not here, as the French proverb has it, plenty of cats for you to comb? And isn't it just here, in the new foothold it gives you, the new clear vision and certitude—in its noble, serious, and invulnerable faith—that mysticism is "useful"; even for the most scientific of social reformers, the most belligerent of politicians, the least sentimental of philanthropists?

To "bring Eternity into Time," the "invisible into concrete expression"; to "be to the Eternal Goodness what his own hand is to a man"—these are the plainly expressed desires of all the great mystics. One and all, they demand earnest and deliberate action, the insertion of the purified and ardent will into the world of things. The mystics are artists; and the stuff in which they work is most often human life. They want to heal the disharmony between the actual and the real: and since, in the white-hot radiance of that faith, hope, and charity which burns in them, they discern such a reconciliation to be possible, they are able to work for it with a singleness of purpose and an invincible optimism denied to other men. This was the instinct which drove St. Francis of Assisi to the practical experience of that poverty which he recognised as the highest wisdom; St. Catherine of Siena from contemplation to politics; Joan of Arc to the salvation of France; St. Teresa to the formation of an ideal religious family; Fox to the proclaiming of a world-religion in which all men should be guided by the Inner Light; Florence Nightingale to battle with officials, vermin, dirt, and disease in the soldiers' hospitals; Octavia Hill to make in London slums something a little nearer "the shadows of the angels' houses" than that which the practical landlord usually provides.

All these have felt sure that a great part in the drama of creation has been given to the free spirit of man: that bit by bit, through and by him, the scattered worlds of love and thought and action shall be realised again as one. It is for those who have found the thread on which those worlds are strung, to bring this knowledge out of the hiddenness; to use it, as the old alchemists declared that they could use their tincture, to transmute all baser metals into gold.

So here is your vocation set out: a vocation so various in its opportunities, that you can hardly fail to find something to do. It is your business to actualise within the world of time and space—perhaps by great endeavours in the field of heroic action, perhaps only by small ones in field and market, tram and tube, office and drawing-room, in the perpetual give-and-take of the common life—that more real life, that holy creative energy, which this world manifests as a whole but indifferently. You shall work for mercy, order, beauty, significance: shall mend where you find things broken, make where you find the need. "Adoro te devote, latens Deitas," said St. Thomas in his great mystical hymn: and the practical side of that adoration consists in the bringing of the Real Presence from its hiddenness, and exhibiting it before the eyes of other men. Hitherto you have not been very active in this matter: yet it is the purpose for which you exist, and your contemplative consciousness, if you educate it, will soon make this fact clear to you. The teeming life of nature has yielded up to your loving attention many sacramental images of Reality: seen in the light of charity, it is far more sacred and significant than you supposed. What about *your* life? Is that a theophany too? "Each oak

doth cry I AM," says Vaughan.   Do you proclaim
by your existence the grandeur, the beauty, the intensity, the living wonder of that Eternal Reality within which, at this moment, you stand?
Do your hours of contemplation and of action
harmonise?

If they did harmonise—if everybody's did—
then, by these individual adjustments the complete group-consciousness of humanity would be
changed, brought back into conformity with the
Transcendent; and the spiritual world would be
actualised within the temporal order at last.
Then, that world of false imagination, senseless
conflicts, and sham values, into which our children
are now born, would be annihilated.   The whole
race, not merely a few of its noblest, most clear-
sighted spirits, would be "in union with God";
and men, transfused by His light and heat, direct
and willing agents of His Pure Activity, would
achieve that completeness of life which the mystics dare to call "deification."   This is the substance of that redemption of the world, which all
religions proclaim or demand: the consummation
which is crudely imagined in the Apocalyptic

dreams of the prophets and seers.   It is the true
incarnation of the Divine Wisdom: and you must
learn to see with Paul the pains and disorders of
creation—your own pains, efforts, and difficulties
too—as incidents in the travail of that royal birth.
Patriots have sometimes been asked to "think im-
perially."   Mystics are asked to think celestially;
and this, not when considering the things usually
called spiritual, but when dealing with the concrete accidents, the evil and sadness, the cruelty,
failure, and degeneration of life.

So, what is being offered to you is not merely a
choice amongst new states of consciousness, new
emotional experiences—though these are indeed
involved in it—but, above all else, a larger and
intenser life, a career, a total consecration to the
interests of the Real.   This life shall not be abstract and dreamy, made up, as some imagine, of
negations.   It shall be violently practical and
affirmative; giving scope for a limitless activity of
will, heart, and mind working within the rhythms
of the Divine Idea.   It shall cost much, making
perpetual demands on your loyalty, trust, and self-
sacrifice: proving now the need and the worth of

that training in renunciation which was forced on you at the beginning of your interior life. It shall be both deep and wide, embracing in its span all those aspects of Reality which the gradual extension of your contemplative powers has disclosed to you: making "the inner and outer worlds to be indivisibly One." And because the emphasis is now for ever shifted from the accidents to the substance of life, it will matter little where and how this career is actualised—whether in convent or factory, study or battlefield, multitude or solitude, sickness or strength. These fluctuations of circumstance will no longer dominate you; since "it is Love that payeth for all."

Yet by all this it is not meant that the opening up of the universe, the vivid consciousness of a living Reality and your relation with it, which came to you in contemplation, will necessarily be a constant or a governable feature of your experience. Even under the most favourable circumstances, you shall and must move easily and frequently between that spiritual fruition and active work in the world of men. Often enough it will slip from you utterly; often your most diligent

effort will fail to recapture it, and only its frag-
rance will remain.   The more intense those contacts have been, the more terrible will be your
hunger and desolation when they are thus withdrawn: for increase of susceptibility means more
pain as well as more pleasure, as every artist
knows.   But you will find in all that happens to
you, all that opposes and grieves you—even in
those inevitable hours of darkness when the doors
of true perception seem to close, and the cruel
tangles of the world are all that you can discern
—an inward sense of security which will never
cease.   All the waves that buffet you about, shak-
ing sometimes the strongest faith and hope, are
yet parts and aspects of one Ocean.   Did they
wreck you utterly, that Ocean would receive you;
and there you would find, overwhelming and transfusing you, the unfathomable Substance of all
life and joy.   Whether you realise it in its personal or impersonal manifestation, the universe
is now friendly to you; and as he is a suspicious
and unworthy lover who asks every day for renewed demonstrations of love, so you do not
demand from it perpetual reassurances.   It is

enough, that once it showed you its heart. A link of love now binds you to it for evermore: in spite of derelictions, in spite of darkness and suffering, your will is harmonised with the Will that informs the Whole.

We said, at the beginning of this discussion, that mysticism was the art of union with Reality: that it was, above all else, a Science of Love. Hence, the condition to which it looks forward and towards which the soul of the contemplative has been stretching out, is a condition of *being*, not of *seeing*. As the bodily senses have been produced under pressure of man's physical environment, and their true aim is not the enhancement of his pleasure or his knowledge, but a perfecting of his adjustment to those aspects of the natural world which concern him—so the use and meaning of the spiritual senses are strictly practical too. These, when developed by a suitable training, reveal to man a certain measure of Reality: not in order that he may gaze upon it, but in order that he may react to it, learn to live in, with, and for it; growing and stretching into more perfect harmony with the Eternal Order, until at last, like the blessed ones of Dante's vision, the clearness of his flame responds to the unspeakable radiance of the Enkindling Light.